Dear Becky, I hope you *enjoy* this book! It does have lots of ideas. The ideas starts with spending time together. Even tho we are miles apart, I hope you know that I will always be nea 2016 - Enjoy Birthday week - [illegible]

9 **WHISKS**
5 **PACKS OF PASTA**
1 **DUCK PRESS**
3 **PACKS OF COFFEE**
22 **KNIVES**
6 **HALF-EMPTY PACKS OF COUSCOUS**
8 **SAUCEPANS**
92 **DIFFERENT KINDS OF TEABAGS**
14 **WINE GLASSES**
8 **MILK GLASSES**
7 **JUICE GLASSES**
1 **PAIR OF GLASSES...**

Finally! I've been looking for ages!

What's for dinner?

At IKEA, when we talk about creating a better everyday life, we really mean creating solutions that will help life run more smoothly.

Making life easier. More fun. More free. In our previous book, FIND IT! Part 1, Clothes and Shoe Storage in Eight Homes, we had a look in people's wardrobes and shoe cabinets. This time we've visited some new families and looked in their kitchen cabinets, opened their drawers and checked out their fridges and pantries. We've sat down to eat with them and been part of their lives related to food and the kitchen. We've also been given their favourite recipes, which are all different but just as delicious. After all, life in the kitchen is more about the food than the cabinets. Spending time together round the table is where it all begins: the chats and the crumbs, the laughs and the arguments, the mess and the sulking, the giggling and the silence at the dining table. Well, we say dining table but a lot of us eat in front of the computer, on the sofa, in bed, in the bath or on the way to work. For most of us though, at some point in our lives, meals go from something we rush, to something we slow down for. One of the highlights of the day. An opportunity to gather and share something valuable – everyday life. With this book, we aim to inspire you in how you can store things in the kitchen. We take a look at ten different homes and how their kitchens are organised. Because before you actually sit down, the food has to be prepared, or collected. So how can you make that just as enjoyable as the actual meal? With a kitchen you can find things in. A kitchen that has a favourite frying pan close to the cooker, and a really sharp knife within easy reach. A kitchen that perhaps provides a nice bit of daylight, and some planning that makes both cooking and washing up afterwards an actual pleasure.

A kitchen that helps you focus on the food. Because that's where everything begins. So, what's for dinner? Me, I'll be having a nice salad and pasta with pesto. Would you like my recipe? Here you go!

Mia Lundström
Creative Director Home Furnishing
IKEA of Sweden

Mia's pesto

The world's easiest and probably the world's tastiest pesto. You can also very it depending on what you have in the fridge or garden.

Serves 6

100 g wild garlic
100 g parmesan cheese, grated
100-200 ml rapeseed oil
salt and pepper
freshly squeezed lemon juice
100 ml almonds

Blend everything in a food processor. Season. Serve.

Keeps in the fridge for several days.

You can fully or partially replace the wild garlic with basil, parsley, rocket or a mixture of all of them.

The parmesan can be replaced by any mature hard cheese.

Instead of almonds you can use pine nuts, cashews or hazelnuts.

Experiment and find your favourite version!

Mia's Pesto

The great(est) workplace.

Over the years, I've had the privilege of visiting countless kitchens. Partly as a guest, obviously, but as a food journalist I've also worked in everything from cramped little kitchenettes to the most extravagant restaurant kitchens. The only kitchens I don't really like are ones that seem to be dedicated to something other than their true purpose: preparing food.

Because let's face it, a kitchen is all about food and food preparation. Even though our kitchens have to fit in so much more than efficient food preparation – lazy Sunday breakfasts, dinner with friends and everyday family life – food is what this space is all about.

Whether you cook a lot and often or a little and rarely, the kitchen is the greatest workplace in the home. Nowhere else do we need to store so much stuff and so many utensils and appliances, ideally all easily accessible whenever we need them. Even in the most basic of kitchenettes there are at least 50 or so items, and in the home of an ordinary food-loving family there could be thousands if you count all the zesters, measuring sets and shellfish knives.

Of course there's nothing to stop us looking at the true professionals – the chefs – and borrowing some smart ideas from restaurant kitchens. They are generally organised so that whatever is used most is most easily accessible, while all the work surfaces are kept free. However, planning a home kitchen is actually more complicated than organising a restaurant one. For instance, at home we rarely have the luxury of a separate washing-up room or a separate cooker just for making sauces. Also, cosiness is rarely a high priority in a restaurant kitchen.

Even so, planning your ideal kitchen always starts with the question: What kind of cook are you?

Do you love preparing food from scratch, baking sourdough bread and stuffing your own sausages? If so you need to leave plenty of space for a food processor, large bowls and all kinds of saucepans.

Are you like me, a spontaneous cook who rarely follows recipes down to the finest detail? Keep a few inspiring ingredients and spices out and they're sure to end up in some meal or other quite soon.

Try moving things round a bit. Who says cutlery has to be in the top drawer? How often do you actually use the utensils that have pride of place next to the cooker?

I personally have five balloon whisks there, which is probably a bit more than I need. But then again, I do like to make the occasional spontaneous hollandaise sauce…

Anna Michelson
Food journalist

kitchen

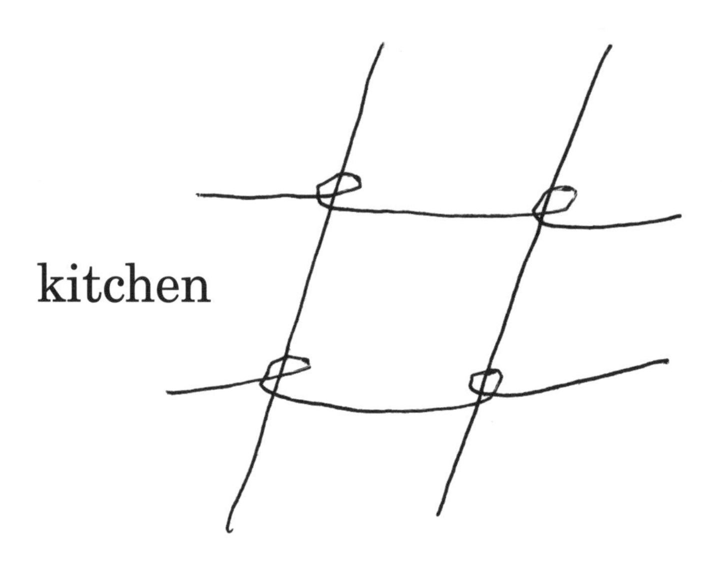

one

Jenny, Johan, Ellen and Esther

This must be one of the cosiest places to eat breakfast in the capital. Have a seat in this sunny little kitchen, at the table full of crumbs where the whole family are gathered – Jenny and Johan and Ellen and Esther. The family are happy here, and they're experts at the art of enjoying life. They live in quite a small space, but at the weekends they escape the city to their summer cottage by the sea, where they can breathe fresh air and smell the aromas of the forest. But they spend their everyday lives in this warm, creative home, full of unconventional solutions and delightful ideas.

To make the best use of the available space, they've built wall cabinets right up to the ceiling. At the very top is the stuff they rarely use, and they need a ladder to reach it.

They eat breakfast and dinner in the kitchen. But when they have guests they sit in the big room, where the dinner table shares the space with Jenny and Johan's bed. There are also books, magazines and a nice cabinet of curiosities here. The room serves all kinds of purposes, but feels calm and inviting thanks to the consistent colour scheme and creative environment. The balcony and windows help keep the room light and airy even though it's a combined bedroom, living room, dining room and office space.

The home comprises a kitchen, the girls' bedroom and a big room where Jenny and Johan sleep, the family eat when they have guests, socialise and watch TV.

BOURGOGNE
PINOT NOIR
ZINFANDEL
Côte Du Rhône
LENTIL
SOUP

Next to the kitchen table is a shelf unit for everyday crockery, napkins and plates. They hang the most frequently used utensils on the wall above it. The wall is painted with blackboard paint.

An old black-painted cabinet holds all the family's cookbooks. On top are their everyday foods: muesli, cereals, crisp rolls, chocolate powder, tea and coffee. There's no point putting them in the cupboards – there's neither room for them nor time in the morning!

The same principle applies to glasses and cutlery. They're always out on the table in nice jars.

BOURGOGNE
PINOT NOIR
Côte Du Rhône
LENTIL
SOUP
SAVON
DE

Above the sink they have all their everyday glasses, cups and mugs.

THE NATURAL
APOTHECARY
GREEN KITCHEN STORIES & DRY PRESENT

Jenny's American pancakes

The whole family lead hectic lives with work and school, laundry and homework. So when the weekend comes, they have a lie-in and make American pancakes with all kinds of unhealthy toppings. They're great, give them a try!

makes about 8 pancakes

350 ml plain flour
2 tsp baking powder
1/2 tsp salt
2 tbsp sugar
1-2 tsp vanilla extract
peel of 1 lemon
2 tbsp butter
250 ml milk
1 egg
butter for frying

Mix the flour, baking powder, salt, sugar, and grated lemon peel in a bowl.

Melt the butter, beat it with the milk, egg and vanilla extract and add to the bowl of dry ingredients.

Fry the pancakes in a medium-hot frying pan until golden brown.

Serve with warm syrup and blueberries, or whatever your favourite fresh berries might be.

1

2

3

4

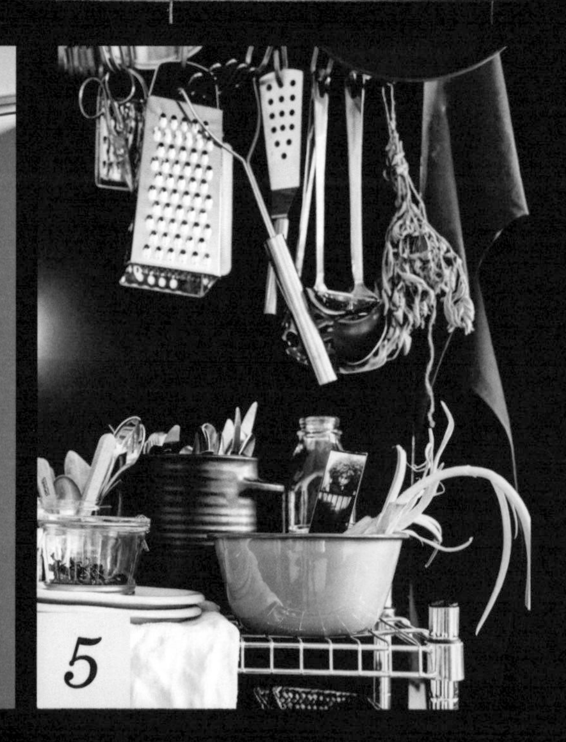

5

Small spaces, small children, very small breadcrumbs – how do they mix? Very well! A home where you all share a limited space obviously needs to be functional, but you need to be able to make your own mark on it too. Solutions that reflect who you are and how you live are often very smart and work very well – for you.

1

The shelves in the fan cupboard may be shallow, but there's room for dried spices and tea.

2

When it comes to kitchen appliances, sometimes you need to ask yourself what needs to be out all the time and what doesn't. Jenny and Johan use the blender daily for smoothies, and the juicer on weekends when they make their own vegetable juice.

3

There's a hidden washing-up rack in one of the wall cabinets, ideal when you're short of space. The morning washing up can be there drying, and your worktop isn't full of cups and bowls.

4

Jenny likes to use transparent plastic pots so she can easily see what foods they have at home and how much couscous and pumpkin seeds they have left, for example. This way they avoid buying couscous again and then realising there are already four packs in the cupboard,hiding behind the basmati rice.

5

Do you have more utensils, pans and plates than kitchen cabinets? Add an extra shelf, put up a shelf on the wall, hang some of the utensils on the wall. Think outside the box!

kitchen two

Per

How small can a kitchen be, but still work? As in a kitchen with a fridge, freezer, cooker and somewhere to wash up? A kitchen with room for some crockery and some food? We may have found the very smallest fully equipped kitchen in the world. On just half a square metre of floor space, Per has used surgical precision to fit in all the functions of a big kitchen. Ready? Breathe in and squeeze into this exclusive little kitchen.

RANCILIO

The kitchen is an old wardrobe that's 1.20 metres wide by a full 3.20 metres high. But a lack of space certainly doesn't have to mean a lack of quality. Good choice of materials, discreet colours and intelligent use of the space have transformed this cubicle to a luxurious little mini kitchen. Full use has been made of the ceiling height by building cupboards all the way up to the cornice. The left-hand cupboard hides a carbon filter fan to keep the apartment free of cooking fumes.

Per has no conventional oven but a built-in microwave. Everyday plates are kept above the microwave, and above the fan cupboard are the fine china and wine glasses.

We often choose light colours in small spaces to make them seem bigger. Per did the opposite. Based on the grey of the cabinet doors, he kept the colour scheme somewhat exclusively dark, with a grey stone floor and a black stone worktop. He did however opt out of tiles, as the squares would make the small wall surface too busy. Instead the wall is painted with a grey wipeable paint.

GRANOLA

ICA
Makaroner
Makaroni
Winborgs
ÄTTIKSPRIT
12%
500g
e 1 kg

The small pantry is to the right in this mini kitchen. The shelves are positioned according to pack sizes. At the top are rarely used items. There's very little space, but Per has still left room for your hand to grab the containers.

There's also a small under-counter fridge with a great freezer compartment. The fridge may be small, but it fits in a lot more than you'd think. It goes right down to the floor and has two good vegetable drawers at the bottom.

Under the sink there's a drawer for washing-up stuff and recycling. A light comes on when you open the drawer, a nice little effect in an otherwise quite unglamorous drawer.

Breakfast, especially the morning coffee, is absolutely crucial here. Per likes to quote his old gran Alma – "Coffee is the best of all earthly beverages" – and finds the aroma of freshly ground coffee beans unbeatable! Per has invested in a high-end coffee machine and always has excellent coffee at home. However, there was no room for the fine coffee machine in the kitchen, so it's on a small trolley with everything else that didn't fit: a blender, crisp rolls to have with the coffee, cups and mugs, teapots, thick and thin china, smoothie glasses, grains and cereals. At the bottom are big saucepans and other large utensils.

RANCILIO

Per's super-smoothie

Need to replenish your energy after looking at all these ideas about kitchens? Try Per's super-smoothie. It's amazingly tasty, amazingly healthy, easy to make and even looks good!

2 servings

400 ml raspberries
2 tbsp hemp seeds
1 mango, ripe
100 ml oat milk
100 ml granola

Topping

1 pomegranate lemon balm

Blend the raspberries and hemp seeds in a blender. Rinse, and then blend the mango and oat milk. This is done to separate the raspberry and mango colours. Put a couple of tablespoons of the raspberry mix into the bottom of a glass. Layer on some granola, and then some mango mix. Top off with pomegranate and lemon balm.

This will make two glasses.

1
2
3
4
5
6

Thinking about building a small kitchen at home? If you want inspiration, forget fancy interior design magazines. Instead take a look at a friend's camper van or your grandad's boat – places that really know how to make the most of every space.

1

If you're building a mini kitchen maybe you can treat yourself to high-quality materials, since you won't need that much of them. Per went for a black granite worktop without breaking his budget.

The tap is black to blend into the black worktop, but the handles are brass to further reinforce the exclusive feel of this small kitchen.

2

Per arranged the shelves in his small pantry cupboard according to the height of the packs. Need more room in your cupboards? Eliminate wasted space!

3

The magnetic knife rack is home to all kinds of everyday items, from scissors and a salt pot to a corkscrew and various knives. Keeping a lot of everyday stuff on the magnetic rack freed up a whole drawer in the kitchen.

4

Underneath the wall units, Per has put up a deco strip to frame the cabinets nicely and conceal the built-in LED lighting. Rather than a standard large oven, Per has chosen a microwave which suits the small kitchen well.

5

The kitchen cabinets are slightly higher up than normal. It's 65 cm from the worktop to the bottom of the wall units, rather than the standard 55 cm. The ten extra centimetres add space and airiness to the kitchen, and also leave space for a small shelf. Even with little space, it's good to try and give it some sense of airiness. It makes the surface less compact.

6

The bar on the wall has room for utensils and a washing-up brush. When it's washing-up time you just hang the fold-out rack on the bar and take out the small sieve for the sink. There was no room for a dishwasher.

Åsa

In the middle of the city, in an elegant stairwell, we meet Åsa. She's a devilishly good cook and enjoys military order in her cupboards and drawers. The door is always open, and if a group of hungry friends drop by she never gets stressed – quite the opposite in fact. "Well hi! Come on in, great to see you, fancy a glass of wine?" But then she does have something of a super-kitchen with loads of space, a luxury island and copious amounts of storage. Come on in if you like very good order, even better pizza and a really good laugh.

Maximum use has been made of the apartment's ceiling height, and Åsa has double wall cabinets right up to the ceiling. Being neither very tall nor very strong, Åsa keeps things she uses only very rarely on the top shelf of the top cupboards: colourful little mugs, stubby vases, party decorations, false beards, non-matching carafes, streamers and crazy serving dishes inherited from her grandmother. She has a ladder to help her reach – it's always out, and is an absolute must for the idea of double wall cabinets to work.

On the worktop is a dish of lovely honey tomatoes and all the important seasonings. She often buys fresh produce from the local market, and likes to leave her purchases on the worktop until she uses them. Function becomes decoration.

Åsa's great passion is having dangerously sharp knives. There's an impressive collection in the top drawer. The plasters are in the next drawer along.

Åsa doesn't like heavy lifting, so she keeps her well-used copper saucepans (which she got from her brother, a chef) at the top of the drawer next to the cooker.

This is a real dream kitchen, which transitions into a dining area, which transitions into a living room. It's quite simply a big, spacious room that's a kitchen, dining area and living room in one.

Although the apartment's on the ground floor, it's light because it has several high windows looking out onto the street.

The dining area is in the middle of the room, with the large storage wall on one side and the bookcase on the opposite wall. To soften the home up a bit there's a lovely big linen tablecloth on the dining table.

Åsa has chosen to build a classic pantry with a modern twist. It's between the oven and the fridge to separate hot and cold. It's home to beans, chickpeas, fine olive oil, vinegar and tinned tomatoes. Here too, good order is vital. Dry products in their own space, and wet ones in theirs. None of this runny honey next to the flour. And of course it should look appealing when you open the pantry, so there's no ugly packaging!

The kitchen has a steam oven which is great for cooking vegetables. Åsa has also equipped the oven with a baking stone which gives her delicious pizzas the right taste, consistency and crispiness.

The fridge door is where you'll find a variety of seasonings that Åsa always makes sure she has in: port, sherry, bouillon, French mustard and white cooking wine.

The island links the food preparation with the social aspect of the kitchen. It's a place for cleaning, cutting and chopping, somewhere to get together for a drink before dinner is served. And on an ordinary Tuesday morning, it's somewhere to stand and have breakfast.

And because the island is close to the cooker, it's also a good general surface for putting hot pans and baking trays.

Åsa is an epicurean who never cuts corners with food. Food and wine are important ingredients in her life. She comes from a family that has cooking in their blood and her close relatives run several fine restaurants in the city. She either cooks at home or eats out at some very good restaurant.

When she's cooking, getting the best ingredients is tremendously important, and she devotes a lot of time and care to finding the right products. She goes to food markets and wholesale markets to carefully select what will end up on the dinner table. Åsa does have a good many cookbooks but she never cooks to a recipe, preferring to create her own variations.

Åsa's gourmet pizza

When you have a steady stream of guests like Åsa, it's a good idea to serve something that everybody likes. Åsa's gourmet pizza may even go down in history as the best in town. The secret? Having a lot of fun when you're making it!

Serves 4

Pizza dough

50 g fresh yeast
800 ml flour
300 ml water
about 1/2 tsp salt
2 tbsp olive oil

Dissolve the yeast in the water at 37ºC. Add the flour, salt and olive oil. Mix the dough by hand or in a food mixer. Knead the dough well for about 10 minutes. Make sure it is quite elastic. Place the dough in a large bowl, dust over some flour and leave to rise, covered, for about two hours.

Tomato sauce

2 tins passata
1 tube tomato puree
1 tsp sugar
1/2 tsp salt
50 ml olive oil
black pepper

Boil up the passata with salt, sugar, olive oil and black pepper. Mix in the tomato puree. Simmer and reduce for about 20 minutes on a low heat. Season.

Use your favourite toppings on the pizza. Åsa's gourmet pizza has tomato sauce, butternut squash, fresh mozzarella, a tasty hard cheese, a bit of blue cheese, kale, pine nuts, pomegranate seeds and rocket.

Slice the squash thinly, chop the kale (removing the thick stalks), toast the pine nuts and prepare the pomegranate seeds.

Roll out the dough and spread on some tomato sauce. Lay on the squash, crumble over the blue cheese and the drained, sliced mozzarella along with the coarsely grated hard cheese. Cook at the oven's maximum temperature (but no more than 350ºC, for 10-12 minutes.

TIP: Add the kale after half the cooking time so as not to burn it.

To serve: Sprinkle over the pine nuts and pomegranate seeds.

Enjoy!

1

2

3

4

5

6

Åsa loves cooking. But does she love washing up? Less so. We all like a beautiful kitchen with nice cabinet doors, but the flow is actually more important than appearances. When planning where to put the dishwasher, think about where you'll be keeping the glasses, crockery and cutlery. They go together naturally, and your everyday life will be far easier if they live next to each other. Well-considered planning will make all your work in the kitchen a lot easier.

1

A kitchen is so full of stuff that you hardly need decoration. Do what Åsa does and leave tomatoes, onions and spices out on the worktop. If you have a nice bottle of olive oil, leave it on show. If you're having artichokes for dinner, put them in a nice bowl on the worktop.

2

Tidiness is important in the home generally, and especially in the kitchen. The worktop should be free of a load of different appliances, Åsa wants to leave this space free for preparing food. The only appliance she can bear to leave out is the coffee machine in the corner. All other appliances are stored in the island.

3

Åsa has everything she needs to cook right next to the cooker. To make lifting easy she keeps light aluminium saucepans at the bottom, and heavy ones higher up. And at the top in pride of place – her knives.

4

Åsa likes to keep her drawers and cupboards tidy, and ideally the contents should look good too. Use transparent plastic boxes and jars and even porridge oats can look quite glamorous.

5

Root vegetables, potatoes and onions don't have to sit shivering in the fridge, they're better off a tad less cool in the kitchen island.

6

Dried spices are best kept in the dark of a drawer, while fresh herbs prefer a nice sunny window. When the fresh herbs start to wither, you can dry them and put them in a jar.

Gunnel and Dante

Once you get past all the beautiful oak woods and whispering birch trees and carry on right into the greenery and open fields, this is where you'll end up. This is the home of Gunnel and her teenage son Dante, and their cat Findus, in a wonderful old late 19th century school. With a lush garden and an exuberant greenhouse, they have all the food they need just outside the kitchen door. They originally only lived here during the summer, but the forest and tranquillity and the idea of being almost completely self-sufficient for food were so appealing that they moved here full-time ten years ago. Step inside! Hungry? Step outside!

The house is very spacious, but the kitchen is not particularly large and has relatively little worktop and not much storage. But of course that was all a schoolmistress needed at the end of the 19th century. To make more room Gunnel has added wall cabinets above the sink, where the everyday crockery is kept.

To make sure the wall cabinets didn't over-dominate, Gunnel decided to cut them off at the back to make them shallower. So now they are 20 cm deep, but still have room for coffee cups, glasses and some everyday groceries. She has installed LED lights underneath the cabinets which provide good work lighting.

Under the wall cabinets is a bar for hanging all the utensils Gunnel uses most when cooking. The bar also acts as a washing-up rack – water from the newly washed utensils can simply drip down onto the stainless steel draining board.

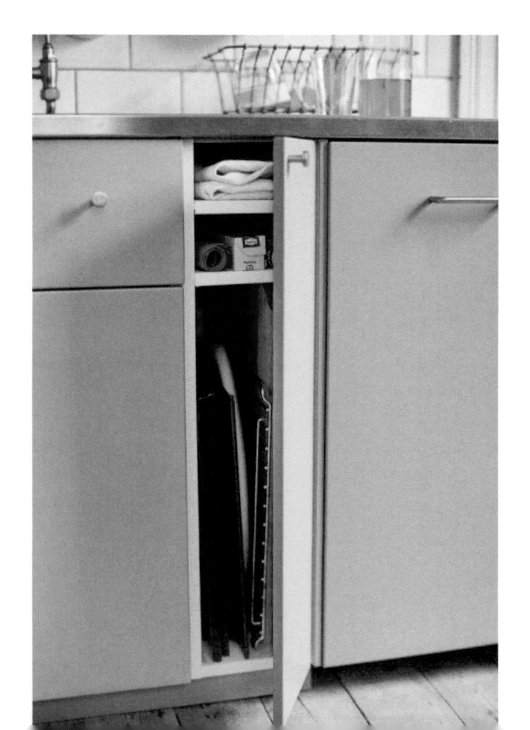

There was a small space over between the dishwasher and under-sink cabinet. Rather than just covering it over, Gunnel managed to squeeze in a 20 cm cabinet where she keeps her pot holders, chopping boards and trays.

The home has a luxurious walk-in pantry where they keep groceries, jam, cordial, dried mushrooms, dry goods, fabric bags and drinks. They also have space for waste separation with glass, metal, paper and cardboard recycling.

The kitchen's colour scheme was determined entirely by this unassuming little school bench. The well-worn and well-chafed painted wooden bench was brought out when the school had visitors or at the end of term. The essence of the bench is now on the walls of Gunnel's kitchen.

Hungry? Gunnel grows tomatoes, chillies, basil and cucumber in her greenhouse. In her vegetable patch she grows lettuce, coriander, parsley, dill, beans, chard, beetroot, asparagus, onions, leeks, cavolo nero, potatoes, broad beans, strawberries, blackcurrants, mint, sage, rocket, radishes, mizuma, sugar snap peas, kohlrabi and carrots.

Gunnel is a designer working mainly with glass, but also porcelain and textile. Meals and drinks are served on her plates and in her glasses.

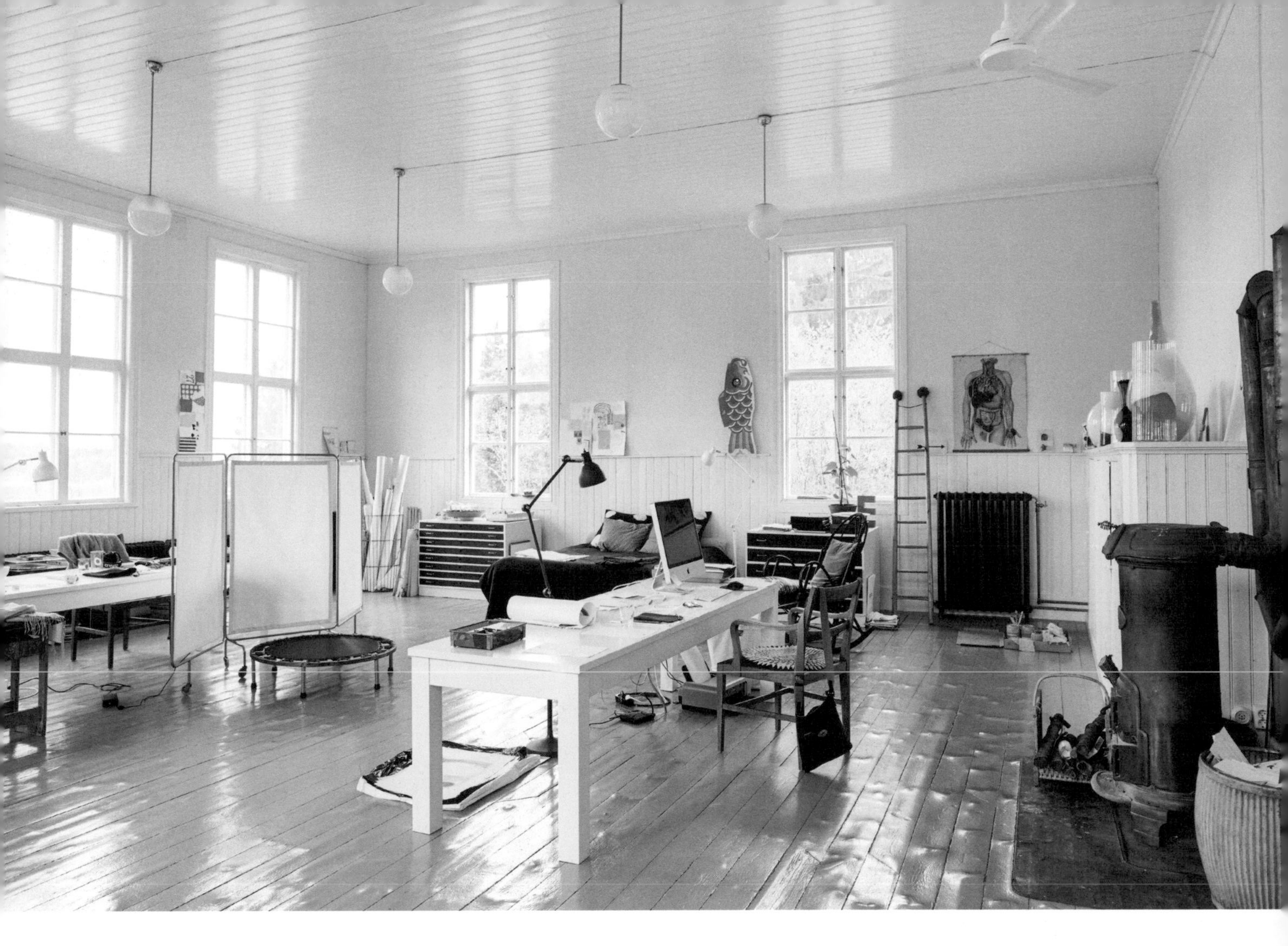

Super luxurious. Imagine having all this space to move around in. Dante and Gunnel share a workroom and have put up folding screens so as not to disturb each other.

All over the house, Gunnel has created beautiful still-lifes of everyday objects. Even a trip to the loo is a beauty-filled experience.

Dante's rhubarb dream

When Dante fancies dessert, he just steps out into the garden and picks some rhubarb. You can of course use rhubarb from the freezer, market or supermarket instead. You'll need to make the panna cotta a couple of hours beforehand.

Serves 6

Panna cotta

300 ml whipping cream
1 vanilla pod
50 ml sugar
2 gelatine leaves

Soak the gelatine leaves in cold water. Cut the vanilla pod lengthways and scrape out the seeds.

Boil up the cream with the sugar, vanilla seeds and pod. Remove the saucepan from the heat. Squeeze excess water from the gelatine leaves and dissolve them in the cream while stirring. Strain, retaining the liquid.

Pour into individual dishes and refrigerate for a few hours.

Serve with the homemade rhubarb compote.

Rhubarb compote

500 g rhubarb
150 ml water
50 ml sugar

Peel and cut the rhubarb into small pieces. Place in a saucepan and mix in the water and sugar.

Boil until the rhubarb is soft. Leave to cool, and then serve.

1
2
3
4
5
6

However long you spend at Gunnel and Dante's place, there's always something new to discover. Exciting books, beautiful ceramics, crazy collections, new shoots in the garden or a nice new cucumber in the greenhouse. The colour scheme is also inspiring. The grey-blue-green shade in the kitchen goes nicely with the white-oiled wooden floors. All the materials have been chosen because they age beautifully.

1

To get exactly the right shade Gunnel blended two different linseed-oil paints – a grey-blue and a green-blue. And to give the colours a little depth, she added a hint of burnt umber to the blend. The walls are in a slightly lighter shade than the cabinet doors to make it look a bit more spacious.

2

Do you need a wall cabinet but think it will take up too much space? Do what Gunnel did: saw it off at the back to make it shallower, but still deep enough for your crockery.

3

Do you have a small storage space that's just waiting to be made into a pantry? Great! Put up shelves for tinned goods, jams and cordials, and keep boxes in there for recycling.

4

Sometimes a small cupboard can make quite a big difference. If you have a few centimetres left over, consider whether you can turn them into storage. Gunnel squeezed in a narrow cupboard under the sink and keeps her trays and pot holder there.

5

Luxury storage! Gunnel's property has a root cellar – storage with an ideal temperature for root vegetables and her own delicious apple cider.

6

The greenhouse, made of white-painted wood, is quite new and provides them with tomatoes and cucumber.

kitchen five

Leonie

This beautiful apartment can be found at the top of a 1920s block. With views of the harbour and nice high ceilings, it is airy, light and spacious.
It's an amazing location, but the kitchen is the real gem in this home. The beautiful original 1929 fixtures and fittings are virtually intact. So when Leonie moved in she decided not to pull down the old interiors and start again, but to keep and preserve as much of the original as possible. But is 1920s function compatible with life in the kitchen today?
Step inside and let's find out.

Tolånga
SMÖR
KÄRNAT AV SYRAD
EKOLOGISK
GRÄDDE

Some homes already have a nice kitchen when you move in, as in Leonie's case. If so, it's worth thinking carefully before renovating. Old carpentry materials are often very high quality. Can you think of a modern kitchen supplier who gives a 90-year guarantee on their units?

Leonie's cooker is in a corner of the kitchen and has no contact with the sink area. She has put a stainless steel worktop to the left so she has somewhere to put things. The top drawer is home to the somewhat uglier ladles and spatulas, while the better-looking ones are left out in the metal pot, obviously.

She has created extra space to put things to the right of the cooker with a stainless steel shelf that was made to measure. Underneath is a good chunky radiator that keeps the tea towels lovely and warm. Above the cooker is a massive hood that was made to measure. The cooker recess may be new, but it blends in well with the rest of the interior.

The cabinet doors are timeless, both in terms of shape and colour. It's when you open the cabinets that you see how far things have progressed.

When this kitchen was built there were no silent self-closing drawers, recessed lighting or smart partitions in the kitchen units. No, these base cabinets have just one wooden shelf. So to increase the functionality of the original cabinets, without demolishing anything, Leonie uses wire baskets and plastic containers to make better use of the space and keep the contents neat and well organised.

The two open shelves above the sink are new. This is where she keeps everyday glasses and crockery easily accessible, along with a few of her favourite things that make her smile.

Leonie has no dishwasher, but she doesn't mind. Because she doesn't do a lot of cooking, the washing up doesn't build up too much. And when she does have to wash up, it's nice and relaxing with the right Charlie Parker track on in the background.

The marble worktop is original. The dimensions are neat and elegant, and go nicely with the simple tiling and the shape of the unit doors. The brass cabinet fittings have been in place since 1929. Well-chosen materials and an understated look have kept this kitchen fresh for almost a century. What a wonderfully sustainable thought!

COFFEE
TEA
SUGAR
FLOUR
500 ML

SPICE
Hoyts
PEPPER BLACK
SPICE
KEEN'S
CURRY
OYAL

There are two old pantries in this kitchen. Behind one door is a fridge freezer. The other pantry is home to all of Leonie's kitchen appliances, all lined up on the shelves. They're in a good place there. She thinks it looks untidy if they're all out, and they also take up a lot of space. The pantry is where they belong, even though some of them haven't been used in a very long time…

ESSENTIAL GARDEN BOOK
JONATHAN ADLER
BELOVED HOMES!
MATERIAL WORLD
HOME
CONTEMPORARY WORLD INTERIORS
SVENSKA KLASSIKER
ONE PLANET

GOOD TO GREAT
JODI PICOULT The Tenth Circle
ALEX GARLAND THE BEACH
AIR BABYLON
KERRY GREENWOOD
Alice Munro
THIS GENERATION HAN HAN
GIRL SAVED KING SWEDEN
SARAH WATERS
PICOULT
the other hand
Three Cups of Tea
FACTORY GIRLS
MALCOLM GLADWELL
MAKE DESIGN MATTER
THE HUMMER AND THE MINI
BRANSON
Richard Branson
Steve Jobs by Walter Isaacson
BRICK BY BRICK
THE LIVES OF JOHN LENNON
BILL BRYSON
CHINA, INC.
I Dream of Madonna
LOGO

LSTERNWIC
ARNEGIE
ST BRIGHTO
A CAULFIEL
VERN BURKE
LEN IRI
AMBERWEL
DEL ST VIA
TOORA
ORRONG

FLOUR
JUG
12

ECIAL
TBALL
COURSE
MALVERN
ING RD
RNWICK
NEGIE
RIGHTON
AULFIELD
N BURKE RD
N IRIS
BERWELL
ST VIA
TOORAK RD
ORRONG RD

Poached egg

Leonie is not a great one for cooking, she works long days and often gets a takeaway from the Thai restaurant round the corner. But when she does cook, she makes the world's best poached eggs. Simple yet refined. The trick is to stay calm and use a really fresh egg.

Serves 1

Ingredients
1 egg
water
1 tsp salt
1 tbsp vinegar

Boil some water. Turn off the heat just as it starts boiling, and add the salt and vinegar.

Break the egg into a cup. Stir up a whirlpool in the water using a spoon. Then pour in the egg, which will stay held together due to the movement of the water. If not, use the spoon to add more motion. Leave the egg in the water a while:

3 minutes for a runny yolk
4 minutes for a creamy yolk
5 minutes for a firm yolk

Lift the egg out with a perforated ladle and transfer carefully to a piece of kitchen roll to drain.

Serve with a little salt, or a few drops of tabasco, or with a salad or a slice of bread.

1
2
3
4
5
6

If you end up in an apartment with nice-looking, but old, kitchen fixtures and fittings, think carefully before reaching for the crowbar. Think about what you can keep and what needs enhancing to make it functional. Leonie kept all the original fixtures and fittings, but made sure to make the insides of the drawers and cabinets functional.

1

If you want to do your own tiling, don't stop at the sink but expand into the room. It's an excellent wall material in a kitchen. Easy to keep clean and very durable.

Leonie was lucky as she found some original tiles in a box in the basement. Are you looking to supplement some old tiling? Look for tiles at flea markets, or in granny's attic.

2

Old kitchen cabinets are rarely considerate enough to be exactly the right size for modern fittings. But think outside the box. Maybe you can adapt a wire basket, or use something that would usually be found in a bathroom cabinet.

3

Want the world's simplest tip? Put knobs or hooks inside pantry doors or high unit doors. You can use them to hang up tea towels, flowery aprons and daft dusters.

4

The kitchen floor is old, but sanding makes it like new.

5

It's always good to have several different kinds of storage in the kitchen. That way, you can adapt the storage solutions to what is actually being stored.

6

This kitchen has a balcony, the ideal place to live it up and eat Sunday breakfast during the warmer times of the year. She also grows a few herbs here, but she brings the pots inside when it gets too chilly.

Liv and Andreas

What do you really need to feel really good in life? Food and love. Or in interior design-ish, a good kitchen and a nice comfy bed. And if you live in a confined space, these are the things you should prioritise – at least that's the opinion of Liv and Andreas, two students who live in a top-floor studio apartment in the city. Rather than having a sad little kitchenette in one corner, they decided to give the kitchen pride of place. So when you open the door to their home on the sixth floor, you're stepping right into the heart of the home: the kitchen. Come on in, we're having balcony-barbecued Arctic char for dinner!

Off with the mittens, on with the rubber gloves. The kitchen is right inside the door. Two steps and you're at the kitchen sink.

Liv and Andreas built the kitchen themselves. Although they made maximum use of all the space, there was no room for a decent-sized freezer. No problem – Andreas has built a large box on the balcony which contains both a chest freezer and storage for outdoor furniture cushions. The lid is made from a piece of copper given to Andreas when he once helped take down an old copper roof.

Both Liv and Andreas are students. Andreas also works as a chef, carpenter and delivery driver – the perfect combination of skills for building a kitchen!

The kitchen is made of good, simple, durable materials. A black laminate worktop, basic white tiles and stainless steel doors.

Instead of painting the walls, they store their food in jars and buy nicely coloured packets that are visually exciting. Want to vary the colours in your kitchen? Vary the colour of the foods you buy!

They have no wall cabinets but use open shelves for their everyday crockery. Everything is out and is used all the time, so it never has time to gather dust. Then again, they don't have that much crockery: four mugs, six wine glasses (the apartment can't accommodate more than six), and bowls and plates for six.

The tiles are smooth white, 15 x 15 cm, which can be found at a good price. They decided to tile all the way up to the cornice to convey a uniform impression.

There's a bar with the most frequently used utensils, and right next to it is Andreas's beloved magnetic knife rack.

Rather than trying to squeeze in a seating group, Liv and Andreas have given the kitchen pride of place in their studio apartment. In one corner is the bed, and next to it is a combined work desk and dining table.

The office is under the bed: a printer, a drawing board and a box of drawing and writing materials. So a workspace is at the top of their wish list. They currently squeeze around the small kitchen table when studying at home.

YOU
HAD
ME
AT
HELLO
SLUSSEN

Valar

The balcony is a lush kitchen where the barbecue plays the lead.

Alice was adopted from a home for stray dogs. Andreas's brother brought her round and Liv and Andreas fell head over heels in love with her, so now she eats and leads a happy life with them.

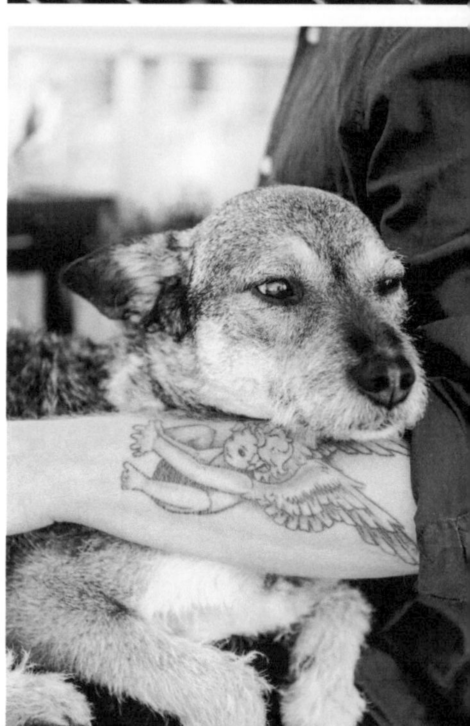

Grilled Arctic char à la Andreas

Don't they have a lovely kitchen? But if Andreas had his way, (virtually) everything would be made on the barbecue. Simple and primeval. And best of all is when he can grill an Arctic char he has caught himself. This is a delicious recipe that also works well with other fish.

Serves 2

caramelised red onion
about 6 red onions, cut into boat shapes
50 g butter for frying
6 tbsp raw sugar
1/2 lemon
pinch of salt

Melt the butter and fry the onions lightly until soft. Add the other ingredients and carry on frying over a medium heat until creamy and marmalade-like. Taste!
Arctic char: Remove the bones. Pull the two sides apart and season with salt and pepper, and fill with herbs, butter and a slice of lemon. Tie the fish with string. Grill on the barbecue.
Mushrooms: Loads of butter. Fry on a high heat. Salt. Use shiitake or chanterelles.
Potatoes: Boil. Drain and snip in plenty of dill.
Brown butter in a frying pan and stir the boiled potatoes around.

1

2

3

4

5

Liv and Andreas live in a studio apartment with a kitchen. Well, actually they live in a kitchen. The kitchen has been allowed to expand as cooking is such a pivotal part of their lives, and the rest of the home has been built around the kitchen. Do you also live in a confined space? What activities are most important in your home? Plan based on activities, not on accepted norms!

1

When they built their kitchen they opted for stainless steel cabinet doors and no floor plinths. They wanted an industrial look with cabinets on visible legs. Cool. But this also appeals to the inner housewife, as it's easy to keep clean.

2

The large zinc box on the worktop is where they keep the bread, and the eggs are left out – they like being in room temperature.

3

The balcony is almost as big as the whole home. As soon as spring comes, they move outdoors. They do almost everything here: cook food, store food, grow food, eat food, work and sometimes just sit and daydream in the sun.

4

All the floors are wooden, but in the kitchen area they've milled out some of the wood and integrated vinyl flooring. The original idea was to have a concrete floor there, but it was too clumsy-looking and complicated. It's smart to have a durable floor that's easy to clean when you're slopping, splashing, spilling and squirting the most.

5

Recycling takes all kinds of forms. Liv and Andreas start in the morning when their very friendly 90-year-old neighbour passes on the newspaper.

They often cycle to the recycling station with newspapers, glass and PET bottles.

Helene, Göran, Ian, Noah and Svea

This 1970s house is full of warmth, joy and loads of food, and is close to the sea, beach and wind. The family share their home with a blind Labrador and their teenage sons' hungry friends. The open-plan solution has created a light, inviting home that makes you want to stay a long time. They have just renovated the kitchen and created a homemaker's dream in green, brass and wood. The grand piano is tuned, the chicken is on the barbecue and the sauces are nearly ready. Can you help set the table?

When Helene and Göran moved in, they decided to remove as many of the old walls as possible to link together the various parts of the home. The result is a ground floor where the hallway, kitchen, living room and dining area become one lovely big space.

They have recently renovated their kitchen, partly because they wanted an even bigger island. The doors are oak and the worktop is cast concrete. The cooker hood, ovens and fridge are stainless steel, while smaller details like handles and shelf brackets are brass. They work well together.

The common theme here is green: green dining table, green vases, green tiles, greens plants indoors and a lot of greenery outdoors.

The cutlery drawer is actually two drawers. The top, slightly smaller one contains the nice cutlery for when the two grandmas come round for dinner. The lower, larger one is home to the everyday cutlery. The kitchen island can be used for a lot – Helene has managed to fit a whole office into one of the drawers.

Svea may be blind, but she can sniff out the drawer that contains all the doggy sweets.

The root of all cooking is… tins! Here the tins have their own box in a drawer – a great use of space if you have quite a high drawer.

Helene brought these bowls home from Grottaglie in Italy. Mixing decorated bowls with monochrome ones is an easy-peasy way of adding a bit of extra vibrancy to your everyday life, and the set table.

They do a lot of carrying between the kitchen and garden. The glass bottles travel in a nice steel basket.

PASQUA
KIVIKS
ASTRAKAN
appelcider

Beer-can chicken

When the sun is shining and the temperature rises, the kitchen moves out into the garden. Their version of beer-can chicken is a fun summer classic.

Serves 4

1 whole chicken, approx. 1.3 kg
1 can of beer, 33 cl
1 sprig fresh rosemary
1 sprig fresh tarragon
a few sprigs fresh thyme
100 g butter
1/2 lemon
50 ml olive oil
salt and pepper
3 cloves garlic
1/2 a chilli, seeds removed

Wash the unopened beer can and then open the whole top using a tin opener. Stick the herb sprigs into the can.

Melt the butter and squeeze the half lemon. Next, rub the chicken with almost all the lemon juice, butter and olive oil. Season generously with salt and pepper on both the inside and outside of the chicken.

Crush the garlic cloves. Pour what's left of the lemon juice into the chicken and push in the crushed garlic and chilli.

Thread the chicken over the can and grill it upright in a kettle barbecue (or other lidded barbecue) for about 1 hour. Grill indirectly, i.e. have the charcoal/briquettes round the sides of the grill. Use a foil tray under the chicken to catch the juices. The chicken is done when the juices at the thickest part of the thigh are clear rather than red. Remove the chicken from the barbecue and leave it to rest for 10 minutes under foil to retain the heat.

Remove the beer can from the chicken and serve with grilled vegetables and some tasty sauces.

1

2

3

4

5

6

When you're planning storage in a kitchen, think about food preparation and serving. Everything to do with the actual food preparation – pans, knives, bowls and ladles – should be kept together. And everything to do with the set table – crockery, glasses, cutlery, candles and napkins – can be kept further away.

1

Flow is important in a kitchen. The kitchen sink and dishwasher make a great team, and they should be near each other to make it easier for you to load the dirty dishes. When they planned the kitchen, this family thought in zones. Near the dishwasher and sink they have crockery and glasses. Next to the cooker they have saucepans, frying pans and everything else they need to prepare food.

2

The raised section of the bar counter is clad with brass, which makes for a delightful transition between kitchen and living room. Even when working in the kitchen they have a full view of what's happening in the rest of the home. They opted for quite a small sink as they hardly ever wash up by hand; crockery, glasses and cutlery move straight on into the dishwasher, which is right next door.

3

Helene has a small home office upstairs, but she usually stands and works at the kitchen island, often in the company of the boys doing their homework. She even has a small office drawer where the keyboard, work papers and the boys' homework go when it's time to start preparing dinner.

4

If you're planning to remove walls, always check that the structure can take it. In this home, the kitchen ceiling needed a supporting column. Rather than hiding it, they painted it in a brass shade.

5

The storage in the island was planned to avoid clashing and having to move when it's time to make dinner. Candles and napkins for the table are kept on the outside of the island. Helene's office drawer is furthest away from the cooker. Knives, small bowls, preparation bowls and chopping boards can be found in the middle.

6

The dog food is in small containers that were actually meant for small bathroom cabinet items – you know, lipstick, cotton buds and so on. But it's your home, so you can put boxes and jars wherever you like. If you can't find what you're looking for in the cook shop, go a bit crazy and check out other storage solutions.

Karin and Peo

After years of living in white homes with white kitchens, Karin and Peo were ready for a black kitchen that exudes more jazz club than cinnamon buns. This couple are passionate cooks who don't take shortcuts with the food, the colour scheme or the way they use the space. Step inside this charming summer cottage that has been transformed into an exquisite, elegant home with bright ideas and dark colours.

They built the kitchen themselves, and spent a lot of time thinking about how they move around in the kitchen when they're cooking, setting the table and washing up. They keep everything to do with food preparation close to the cooker: pans, chopping boards, colanders, ladles and spatulas. The dishwasher is in the island, and the cupboards next to it are for everyday crockery and cutlery.

Although the kitchen is not that big, they have built an island. A kitchen island doesn't have to be an entire continent, it can just be a small island – placed in the middle of the room like this one.

A fridge, freezer and pantry lie concealed behind the black cabinet doors. The drawers in the pantry allow a good overview of what you have in and what needs replenishing.

Leftover dinner becomes lunch the next day. Throwing food away is not an option for Karin and Peo, it's into a small pot and in the fridge with it.

Both Karin and Peo were longing for black unit doors in their kitchen. They had both had enough of white kitchens and were ready for some decadence. There's also a practical consideration: dark colours make the light and white parts even brighter.

The home is not particularly large but is ideal for two adults and a teenage son who lives there half-time. When they bought the house it needed thorough renovation, but rather than keep the original layout Karin and Peo took a flexible approach. They decided to put the kitchen in a slightly smaller room, but it has good light from two directions and you can even get a glimpse of the sea.

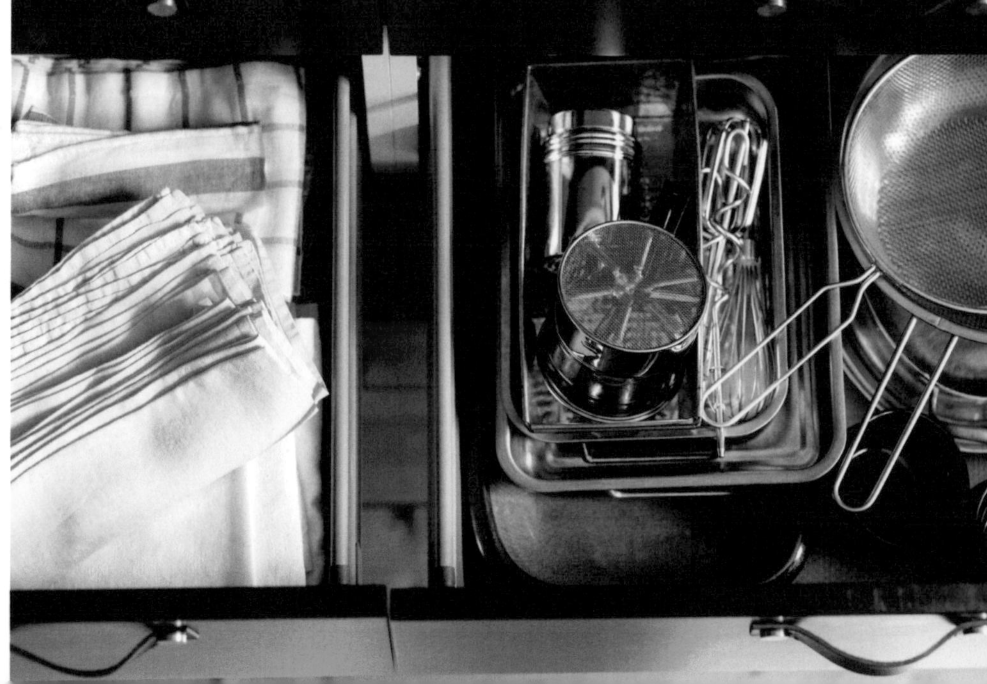

Don't be afraid to combine different metals in the kitchen. At Karin and Peo's place the brass, copper and stainless steel in the kitchen convey a warm, personal impression.

Karin has worked in the glass industry and collects glass from different eras. Drinking glasses combine with bowls and vases and become a nice feature. We ought to add that Karin and Peo have no small children living with them. Kids and beautiful glass don't really mix that well.

An old cabinet in the living room is home to inherited fine china, beautiful serving dishes and a silver coffee pot.

Look familiar? Do you have a drawer like this? One with a very personal, very unclear mixture of cutlery? No one gets what's going on but you.

Peo's Indian meal

Peo and Karin are both keen cooks, but in different ways. Peo always follows a recipe and Karin cooks by intuition. They love Indian food and this is one of their favourite meals. Try making it yourself and you'll be hooked.

Serves 4

Chilli-toasted chickpeas

400 ml cooked chickpeas
2 tbsp toasted chilli flakes
a touch of chilli powder
salt
1-2 cloves garlic
2 tbsp oil

Toast the chickpeas on a high heat. As they start to brown and pop add the oil, garlic and chilli flakes.

Fry on a high heat, stirring all the time. Season with salt before serving.

Serve with raita, bread and a little thinly sliced red onion.

Indian pilau rice

300 ml basmati rice
500 ml water
1/2 tsp salt
1 cinnamon stick
3 whole cardamom pods
1/2 tsp turmeric
50 ml fried onion

Measure out the rice, water and salt and add the cardamom and cinnamon. Use a saucepan with a lid.

Boil the basmati rice covered for about 15 minutes. First bring to the boil on a high heat, and then reduce the heat to simmer until done. Test the rice to make sure it's done. All the water should be absorbed. Remove the rice from the heat and loosen it up with a fork.

Mix the turmeric with a little water in a bowl.

Take about a quarter of the boiled rice and mix it with the turmeric to turn it yellow. Mix the yellow rice with the white. Don't mix it in too much, just enough so there's a bit of yellow rice here and there.

1

2

3

4

5

6

This first thing that strikes you about Karin and Peo's kitchen is that it's black. But perhaps more interesting is the way they've planned their storage. All the food is kept in the tall cabinets. All washing up is done at the island, and all food preparation is done on the long worktop. Colour is one thing, but the key to a functional kitchen is the flow.

1

You don't need a massive kitchen to have an island – it can be a neat little one like this. Karin and Peo's one has the luxury of running water and beautiful daylight. Tempted to build an island in your kitchen? Before getting a hammer and nails out, think carefully and measure, measure, measure!

2

A fridge, freezer and pantry lie concealed behind the black doors. Bring together all food storage – room temperature and cold – in one place and the flow in your kitchen will be more harmonious. It's also quicker to pack the food away in the right place when you get home from the shops.

3

Do you tend to make too much food? Be sure to have pots and jars in various sizes at home to store leftovers. Take a lunchbox to work and save your lunch money for something more exciting.

4

As well as an island, Karin and Peo have a small trolley for keeping utensils in. If you need a free surface and a bit of extra storage, a trolley might be a good idea.

5

Not much room in your pan drawer? Mount a protective plate on the wall and hang them on a bar with hooks like Karin and Peo have done.

6

Peo and Karin decided against conventional handles on their base units and instead had leather straps made, affixed with brass screws. Nice, aren't they? It's also good when there's not much space – you avoid getting caught on protruding knobs and handles as you walk round the worktop.

kitchen nine

Guo Jin, Chen Jian and Chen Mo

Combining a little space with a lot of functionality in a kitchen is a challenge in itself. Add a happy and curious little two-and-a-half year old who can do everything by himself, and... surely that can't work? Actually it does. Chen Jian and Guo Jin's apartment is in the middle of a noisy, busy city. And there's noise and busyness in the kitchen too when young Chen Mo is in the mood to help out. But with two imaginative parents and a well-planned kitchen, life in the kitchen is lots of fun.

不添加香精
不添加防腐
不添加

Maximum storage and functionality in the minimum of space – that pretty much sums up this family's kitchen. It's fully equipped with a rice cooker, microwave oven, oven, hob and washing machine. Putting the oven on the wall gave them a bit of extra worktop space. They've also managed to fit in a small dining area.

功能
Menu
保温
Keep Warm
预约
Panasonic

On the wall are three rows of bars where they hang all their everyday items. The general idea is the less often they use a utensil, the higher up they keep it. Using the walls for storage frees up space in drawers and cabinets. Note that the waste bin is on the floor to make room for other things under the sink.

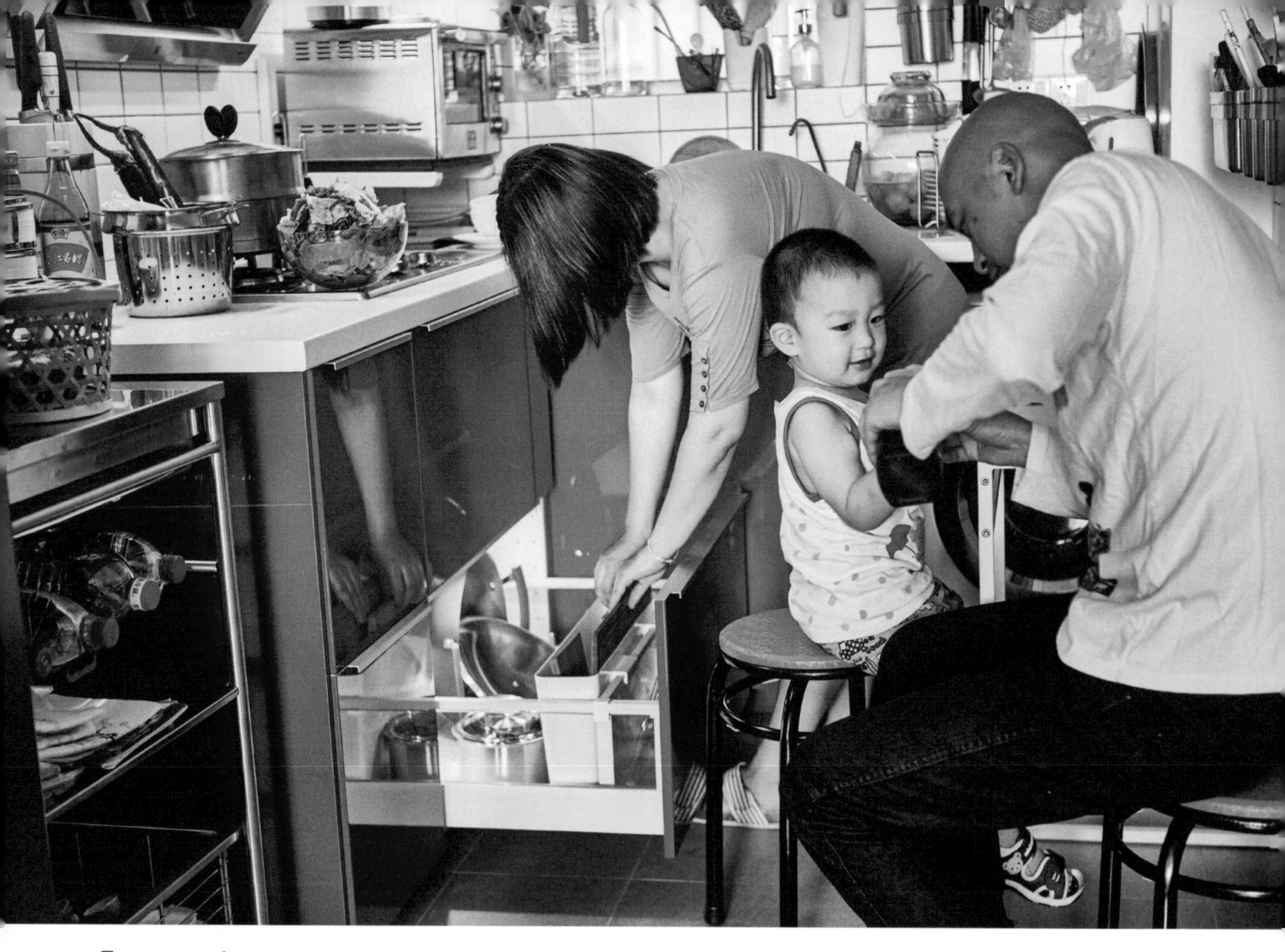

Just as important as being able to find what you need for cooking, is the time you spend together in the kitchen. Talking about minor events and major thoughts while setting the table and preparing the food, well, that's what life's all about.

A really good kitchen trolley should have room for both utensils and drawing stuff. It's also ideal when they need a bit of extra worktop space in the kitchen.

江香醋

州正宗牛
兰州炒饭 炒面 刀削面 土豆烧牛肉盖浇饭
招聘
牛肉水饺

牛
肉

The drawers are home to plates and large bowls. The drawers have integrated lighting, and little Chen Mo loves it just as much every time mum opens them. Open it again mummy!

Chinese cucumber

When the weekend arrives and the family has more time together, they like to make dumplings. With it they serve this lovely cucumber, which goes with most things. Make it with a two year old and it'll take longer, but it will be more fun – especially the banging.

Serves 4

1 cucumber
2-4 spring onions
1-2 cloves garlic
2 tbsp sesame oil
2 tbsp rice wine vinegar
1/2 tsp salt
1/2 tsp sugar
1 tbsp toasted sesame seeds
black pepper

First bang the cucumber with a rolling pin or similar;
this gives it more flavour.
Cut the cucumber lengthways into four.
Cut it into pieces of 1-2 cm.
Finely chop the spring onions.
Grate the garlic cloves.
Mix the garlic with the sesame oil, vinegar, sesame seeds, salt, sugar and pepper.
Mix the cucumber and spring onions with the dressing and leave to stand for 15 minutes or more before serving.

1
2
3
4
5
6

Three people who like cooking and baking, in quite a small apartment – the key here is to be organised, patient and have efficient storage. This little red kitchen is very practical but still has room for some playfulness, which is great when you're a small family.

1

Before you buy even the first little kitchen cabinet, think about the functions and appliances you need to make your everyday life run smoothly. Because Guo Jin and Chen Jian used the walls for a lot of storage, they managed to fit in everything they needed. The high-gloss red doors add warmth to the kitchen and are also easy to keep clean.

2

The dining area is small but just right for this small family. When family come round they put up the other leaf to extend the table. It's crowded, but always nice. They stack their extra stools in the living room.

3

Above the small dining table is an extra shallow cabinet with bowls, glasses and some groceries. Sometimes a deep cabinet is too awkward in a small kitchen and takes up too much space. Here they've trimmed the cabinet at the back to make it shallower.

4

Underneath the cabinet they put up a bar that they hook containers on for chopsticks, other cutlery and a few utensils. This kind of storage hardly takes up any space at all and works in all types of kitchen, whether small or quite a lot bigger.

5

Every space is useable. Don't forget the inside of doors when you're planning a small kitchen, there's room for a lot of stuff here. If you have young children, remember to put child locks on the doors so they can't get to detergents and other dangerous stuff.

6

On the balcony they've put up a shelving system where they store everything from bath towels to soft toys. They also dry their laundry here, so there's always a nice, fresh smell.

kitchen

ten

Ingalill

After more than 40 years abroad at many different addresses, Ingalill has found her dream home. The view is stunning, the colour scheme tranquil and the art exciting. And the kitchen is just the way she wants it – simple, petite and elegant – just like Ingalill herself. After so many years as a nomad, Ingalill is now enjoying a sophisticated home where she can easily invite 20 people to dinner one day and play with her grandchildren the next. But what does a kitchen that's been 40 years in the planning look like? Come inside and see!

Ingalill is a grandmother and is often visited by her two grandchildren Finn and Noël, along with their friend Signe. Ingalill has not childproofed her home. The boys know that at grandma's house they drink from crystal glasses, sit nicely and chat while having a snack, and cut things with sharp scissors.

Because the kitchen wall is slightly angled at the window, Ingalill has had to customise the worktop and cabinet so as not to block the windowsill. The worktop tapers off and she has a narrower base unit closest to the window – a small detail that helps the whole to exude harmony.

This is a very well-planned kitchen. A good kitchen doesn't necessarily have to be big, as long as it's well planned. This one really only consists of a long cast concrete worktop with base units. Simple and effective. To the left of the cooker are the pans, and there are seasonings and fresh herbs on the worktop.

Ingredientes Aceite de oliva
Tuber oligospernum, aroma
Tuber magnatum pico.
AMA BIANCO
ento Agrodolce
sweet Dressing
ITALY R0230
OLIV

Ingalill doesn't actually have that much storage in her kitchen, but it's enough. The more drawers and cabinets you have, the more things you can fit in. But how much stuff do you actually need in a kitchen?

Learn from Ingalill – think first. If you think through what functions you want in the kitchen and where you want them to be, the end result will be better. What kind of cook are you? How many people have to be able to work in the kitchen at the same time? Do you use a lot of appliances? Is a microwave a must for you?

When she has a lot of people round, Ingalill sets the table in her studio. The large, rustic folding table – with an extra leaf in a different colour – is ideal for big dinner parties. Elegant dining tables are great to look at, but not always that practical. Here you can spill a bit of gravy without ruining the table, or the whole evening.

Ingalill's chilli

When Ingalill has people round, she doesn't like to be cooking when they arrive. She prefers to prepare a good stew or casserole in advance and heat it up while they're enjoying an aperitif. Try her chilli – it's exquisite.

Serves 4

2 onions
4 cloves garlic
1 red chilli
1 red pepper
400 g minced beef
butter or oil for frying
2 tsp smoked paprika
1 tsp cumin
1 tsp ground coriander
1 tin chopped tomatoes
200 ml veal stock or other stock
1 orange, zest and juice
1 1/2 tbsp honey
1 tin cooked small white beans
fresh coriander
salt
pepper
light bread
soured cream or natural yoghurt

Start by chopping the onions and garlic, and then finely chop the chilli. Keep the seeds if you want more spice. Cut the pepper lengthways and fry everything in a large saucepan.

Add the minced beef and fry on a high heat. When the meat starts to colour, add the dried spices and carry on frying. Stir regularly to prevent burning. Add the tomatoes and veal stock and cook for 15 minutes until the flavours are concentrated.

Grate the orange zest, squeeze out the juice and add to the pan with the honey.

Rinse the beans in water and add to the pan. Cook the beans for about 5 minutes and top off with chopped fresh coriander.

Season with salt and pepper.

Serve with soured cream or yogurt and bread.

1
2
3
4
5
6

During her years abroad, Ingalill lived at 23 different addresses. Just imagine living with 23 different kitchens; tiny kitchens, far too large kitchens, oddly planned kitchens and hyper-functional kitchens. So when she was planning her own kitchen, she could call on all this extensive experience.

1

Ingalill sorts her waste in the kitchen and empties the containers several times a week. There's a recycling station close to where she lives, and she walks past on the way to the bus. She finds it a good idea to empty the containers often so they don't get too heavy.

2

Do you also have a slightly angled wall in the kitchen? You can actually butcher ordinary kitchen cabinets by cutting them at the back to the right depth. Alternatively, ask a carpenter for help. If you want to be really fancy you can of course build the kitchen on site, but that is usually more expensive. Talk to a kitchen planner before starting.

3

Look closely. There is LED lighting along the floor plinths, which is not only glamorous but also very practical. You have guiding light if you get up in the night for a glass of water, and you add a touch of luxury to your kitchen when it starts getting dark outside.

4

Clever! You can maximise the space in your cabinets by thinking upside down.

5

Want to add some extra personality to your kitchen? Mix old and new. An old cabinet for crockery and a sturdy folding table go well in most kitchens.

6

Ingalill only has four base units (not counting the dishwasher). The crockery is in a separate cabinet. How many cabinets and drawers do you need? Try taking stock of what you have in your drawers and see if there's anything you never use.

Think

smart!

KITCHEN CONJURING!

If you cook in a small kitchen, you know what it's like to long for a free surface to put things on. But where? How? Allow us to present the kitchen conjuror: the kitchen trolley! It gives you an extra surface and an extra workplace, which is also easy to move around. It's also great if your family grows at the weekends – aunts and kids who've left home come to Sunday lunch, and you need a bit of extra space to do the cooking. Conjure forth your trolley and you're sorted.

USE THE WALLS PART 1

Most kitchens have more contents than space, so it's important to be as inventive as possible when it comes to storage. Are your cupboards and drawers full? No need to buy a whole new kitchen – use the wall! This wall has been made into storage for bottles and jars and dried spices. A new shelf on the wall is a simple improvement that also makes you look like a super-chef. And if you want to add some colour to your kitchen, buy attractive new packs in bright yellow and red.

PRAKTISK
IKEA
PLAYING CARDS
JINGPIN PUKE
50 KRONOR

ALARM
LIGHT/SNOOZE
AL ON/OFF
TIME
PLAYING CARDS
SUPERLIM GEL
Handelsbanken
TELIA
MILK
ON THE SPOT

THE DRAWER OF HORROR

What's in here? And how did it get there? Where should it actually be? Don't deny it, we all have a drawer like this in the kitchen. Check out the home of your neatest, tidiest, most well-organised friend – there'll be a drawer from hell there too with all kinds of odd bits in.

WINDOW FARMING!

Just because you live in the city, that doesn't mean you have to forsake a vegetable patch. With a sunny window and a bit of wild thinking, you can transform your window into a mini greengrocers. This book is about storage in the kitchen. So now let us present living storage of food-to-be. Ideally get your children to help plant and harvest your crops, to prove to them that their food doesn't grow in the supermarket.

SORRY!

Think carefully when you're buying food and you can minimise the amount you have left over, or worse have to throw away. How many are eating? Are they children or adults? Measure and weigh carefully. We rarely make too little food… Nice and full? Great! What to do with the leftovers? Tomorrow's lunch!

SHOW OFF!

Not all the food you buy has to go in the fridge. Some things are even better left out. Lettuce often looks tired and withered if it's kept in the fridge too long. Try putting your romaine lettuce in water and see what happens.

TIDY UNDER THE SINK?

A kitchen should ideally look good and smell nice.
But some areas of the kitchen are less attractive.
How can you keep it super-practical, relatively odour-free and also good-looking? Keep the washing-up brush and other washing-up things in their own container.
Also use different kinds of container for different rubbish.
Cardboard can be recycled into new paper products.
Food waste can be composted, and plastic, metal and glass can be recycled.

IKEA

USE THE WALLS PART 2 – KNIFE BONANZA

Cooking shouldn't be dangerous – just pleasant. But if you have your sharp and blunt knives rattling around in the drawer, anything could happen. Free up space in the drawer for something else, and put your knives on the wall.

eko
MELLANMJÖLK
MILD YOGHURT
Sagolika
WAPNÖ
MILD YOGHURT
Bregott
CONFIT
Bregott
eko

FRIDGE VOYEUR

Is it possible to organise a fridge? Absolutely! Start by taking everything out and putting it on a table. Does all of it need to be in the fridge? Some foods are actually better left in room temperature. Tomatoes and onions, avocados and almost all fruits do very well without a fridge. Other foods might be able to move to the freezer. While your fridge is empty, you may as well take this opportunity to give it a good wipe out. A clean fridge uses less energy! Can you move the shelves? Great! That way you can arrange the fridge to suit the foods you have. Do you need space for large pans? Or do you mainly have small packets? Move the shelves around and see what works best for you. Where is the temperature highest? Where is it lowest? Keep your (fridge-proof) vegetables at the top and the things that need the lowest temperatures – milk and cream – at the bottom.

THE MESSY HEART OF THE HOME

Cooking and sitting down together for a nice meal is one of the highlights of everyday life. When the food has been eaten, the conversation is dying and drowsiness starts to set in – the washing up needs doing. Oh joy. If you're planning a new kitchen, or just want to make minor improvements, don't forget the sink area. Try to always have a good draining area to one side of the sink and to have the dishwasher, if you have one, close to the sink. If you can locate the sink by a window and let in some daylight, washing up will automatically feel a little easier.

MAXIMISE YOUR CABINET

Glass-door cabinets are wonderful things to have in the kitchen – they look great and can swallow a lot of stuff. To create even more space, stack the glasses on trays or use special little smart stands. And do you want to keep an eye on where those lovely plates from your auntie are? Place the top one in the stack on edge. This makes the cabinet more interesting, and auntie will be so glad to see her fine china in pride of place.

EVERYTHING YOU WANTED TO KNOW ABOUT KITCHEN ORGANISATION BUT WERE TOO HUNGRY TO ASK

Here are our best tips for organising a kitchen. Whether your kitchen is large or small, new or old, lovely or less lovely, we believe you can find some inspiration here. Already have your perfect kitchen? Excellent! Off you go and take a bath or bake a cake. Everyone else – read on!

THINKING ABOUT BUILDING A NEW KITCHEN? GREAT!

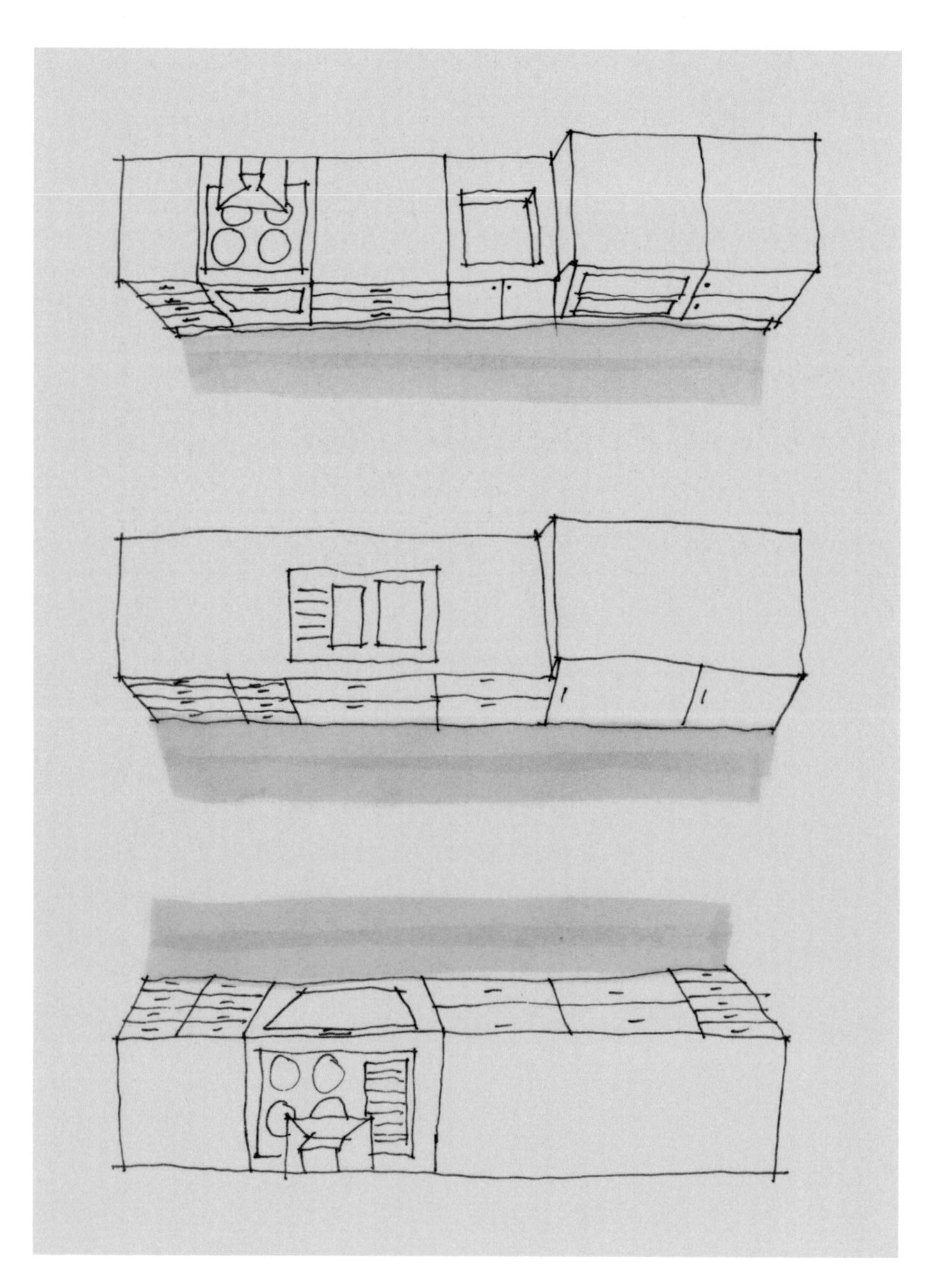

Kitchen sales staff are generally very helpful in advising you how to combine different kinds of drawers and cupboards. But before you get to that stage, think big, and think freely. First of all, which room do want the kitchen in? It doesn't have to be where it's always been.

Depending on the size and shape of the room, think what layout would be best. A U-shaped kitchen, a one-wall kitchen with a long or short worktop, an L-shaped kitchen, or a galley kitchen? A one-wall kitchen can be built in any length, L-shaped is ideal for a small area, while a galley kitchen provides more space. A U-shaped kitchen or one with an island provides a lot of worktop and room for plenty of cabinets. Whichever layout you decide on – think about the golden triangle.

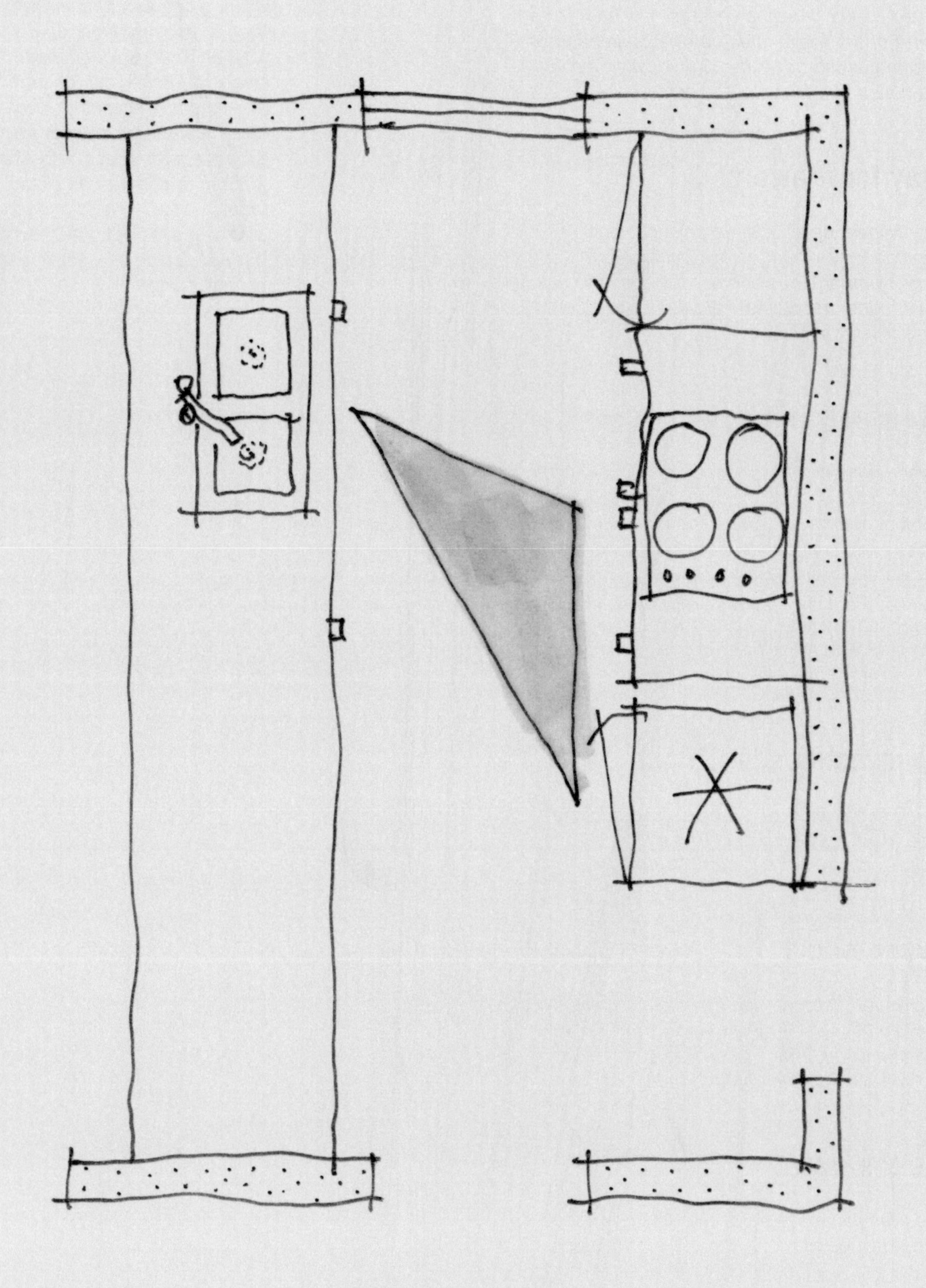

The golden triangle?

Yes, sorry, we mean the relative position of your sink, fridge and cooker. Imagine cooking. You have to get things out of the fridge, stand at the cooker and cook, eat, and then wash up. If the sink, cooker and fridge are positioned in a triangle, the process will be easier.

Hooray for drawers!

If you're wondering whether to have cabinets or drawers under your worktop, we would like to put a word in for drawers. You can use the space so much better with drawers. Drawers also give you a better overview of what's inside.

A few or lots of things?

Build your storage right up to the ceiling and get a sturdy ladder. Plan appliances that are used often in fixed places early on. Think about what kitchen equipment you have, big and small, and how you can store stuff in the best possible way. Strive to have everything as easily accessible as possible.

Avoid deep cupboards that swallow your stuff so effectively that you lose track of it. Drawers generally tend to be better than deep base units.

A top investment – 15 cm

When you're building or refurbishing your kitchen, make the worktop 10-15 cm deeper. The extra few centimetres can swallow loads!

A luxury island

If you can plan your kitchen from scratch, an island or peninsula is invaluable. Even better if the island too has running water. That way two people can work side by side without crowding around the sink.

Raise the oven

Put the oven somewhere else than directly underneath the hob. Ideally place it at chest height in a cabinet – that way you avoid bending down when taking hot things out.

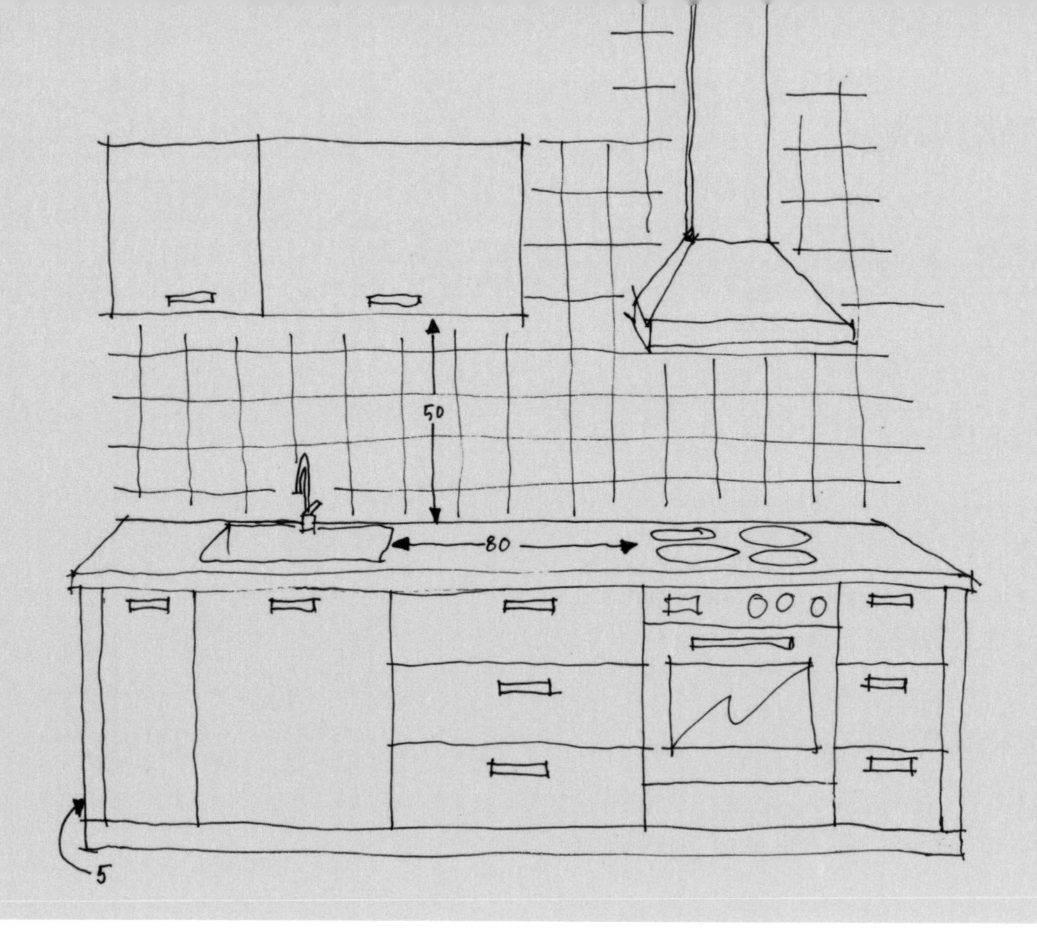

Measure! Measure! Measure!

Precise measuring is crucial when you're baking or cooking, and it's just as vital when you're planning a new kitchen.

The rule of thumb is to have 120 cm of free floor space between cabinet and wall, or cabinet and cabinet, for two people to be able to pass each other comfortably or work side by side. The same dimensions apply for opening the oven or dishwasher door.

You need 50 cm between the worktop and the wall cabinets to allow enough room to work there.

One of the most important dimensions in a kitchen is the size of the work area between the cooker and the sink. If that area is too small, the kitchen will feel cramped even if the room itself is big. If you have room, try to have at least 80 cm between the cooker and the sink. But ideally more. In fact ideally loads more.

Fitting pieces

Bear in mind that the sides of the carcasses can't be placed right up against a wall, as protruding parts like handles, windowsills and curtain rods will get in the way. You generally don't need more than 5 cm to avoid this happening.

Lighting

A room needs several different kinds of lighting: general lighting, work lighting and ambient lighting. Plan light sources and electricity early on. Also make sure you have enough plug sockets for the rice cooker, toaster, electric whisk, espresso machine and computer. For a truly professional effect, you can even install lighting inside your kitchen drawers.

FANCY DOING SOMETHING BIG OR SMALL WITH YOUR EXISTING KITCHEN?

If you have neither the time, money nor inclination to make any major changes, please accept the best tip in the world – move things around inside your cupboards. Think freely, functionally, unconventionally. Or just do a thorough spring clean. Give stuff away that you never use, and chuck out all those spices from the 20th century.

If you want to make a bit more of a change, after spring cleaning you could take down some of your wall cabinets and put up shelves for your everyday crockery.

Another minor but effective way of renewing your kitchen is to buy new knobs and handles for your kitchen units. Bear in mind that handles are best for drawers and knobs for doors.

Put up a picture ledge – perfect for trays and cookbooks.

Buy some nice fridge magnets and remove old timetables and party invitations from the fridge door occasionally.

Clean the fridge. Take everything out. Remove the shelves. Clean the whole lot. Move the shelves around to fit your foods better.

Put up a plate shelf for those extra fine plates.

Sand and oil old wooden worktops. Or go the whole hog and get new ones. Concrete, stone, wood – there are all kinds of exciting materials to choose from.

Get some handy waste-sorting containers you can have under the sink. Use the whole space and don't forget the insides of doors!

Paint a blackboard wall for writing down your daily to-do list.

Replace some cabinets with a glass-door cabinet or open shelving.

Get a kitchen island. They can be small and moveable to create more space, but also as an extra surface to put things on.

A lot of us dream about an old-fashioned pantry with room for everything like jam, cordials, foil, plastic bags, cereals, stock cubes, kitchen appliances, onions, baking powder, tinned foods, cake tins, brooms, light bulbs, plasters and vacuum flasks.

If you have a pantry – lucky you! If you don't, you can actually make one in your drawers or cupboards. You can get dividers or boxes to arrange it all clearly.

Dry goods like flour, sugar, rice and pasta can be transferred to well-sealed jars – that way they'll keep longer.

Keep things that go together, together. Put baking stuff like cocoa, icing sugar and baking powder into a plastic box, and food bags, clips and foil in another. Make a snack box for the kids with chocolate powder and cereals. Or a breakfast box. Or a party box.

ORGANISATION IN THE KITCHEN

Saucepans, utensils and oven dishes need to be near the cooker. Grid shelves are ideal for heavy saucepans and casserole dishes. Hang the utensils you use often on hooks. Hang up a hook rail or bar (or several on top of each other) if there are no wall cabinets. Take care of your knives. They shouldn't be left rubbing against each other. Use a knife tray, a magnetic wall strip or a knife block on the worktop. Invest in a good sharpener and sharpen them regularly.

Olive oils, salt and the herbs and spices you use most can ideally be left out on a tray or in a nice low box.

Keep all your dried spices in a drawer, and ideally use an insert to make it easy to see what's what.

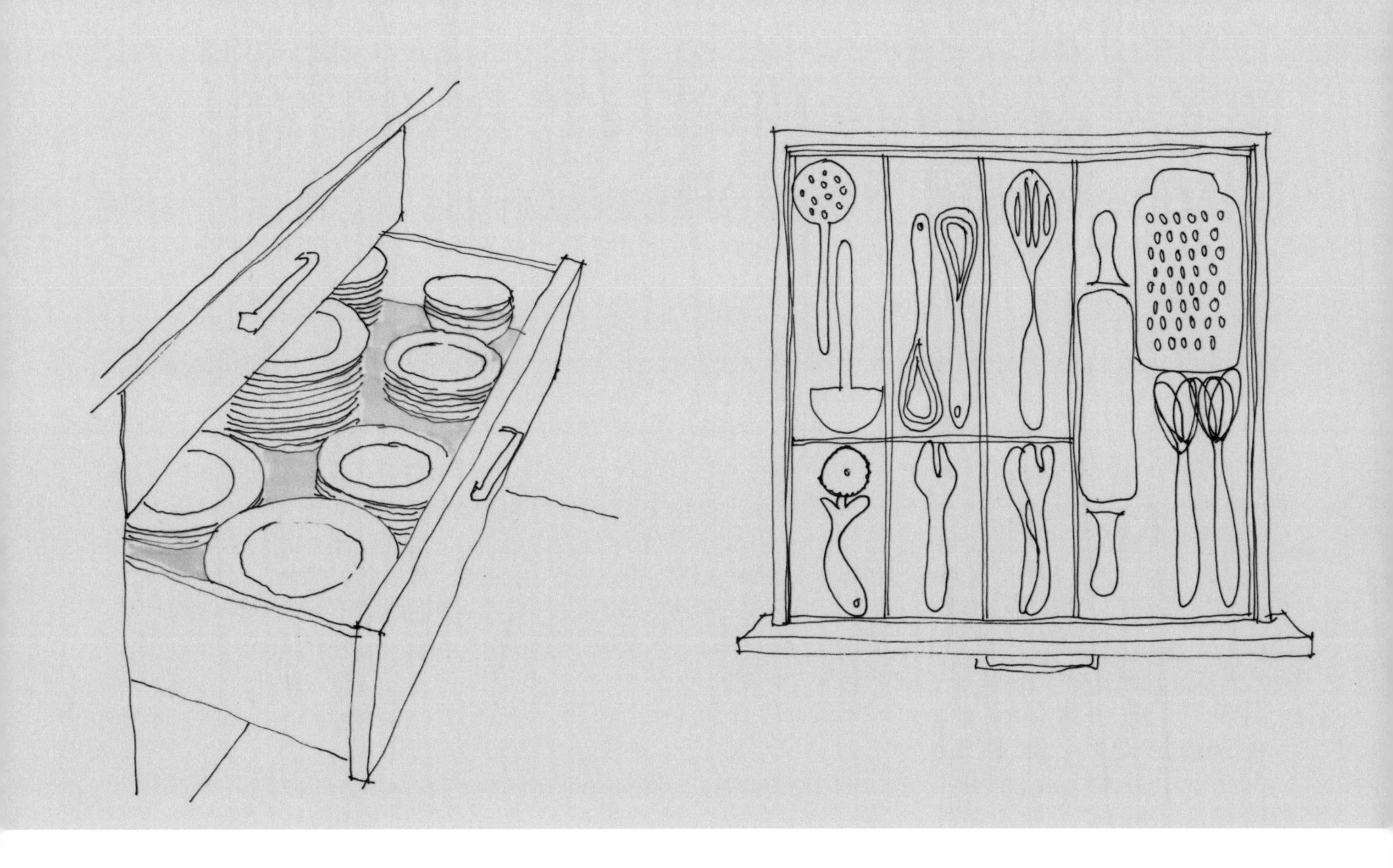

SETTING THE TABLE

Either keep your everyday crockery near the sink and dishwasher, or near your dining area. For added elegance, invest in a small service trolley which you can load the crockery and glasses onto and off of on the way to and from the dishwasher. Want the kids to help set the table? Keep your everyday china in the base units!

AND FINALLY

Clean!

If you have a high, narrow cupboard you can squeeze in a vacuum cleaner, a broom, a first aid box and an ironing board. Finish off with a few hooks inside the door for oven gloves and stained aprons.

Homework, bills and other fun stuff

Plan for activities other than cooking and washing up in the kitchen. The kitchen table is often the hub of the house, somewhere to do homework, pay bills, paint your nails and practise the recorder. Make room for all these other activities in a drawer unit that you can roll out when you need it, or put up a new wall unit to store all your 'non-kitchen' items.

Children in the kitchen

Small children want to be where you are. Clear out a kitchen drawer where they can have toys. Also make sure you have a steady stool they can stand on when they want to help with the cooking. Building a new kitchen? When your children are at their messiest age, it may be a good idea to choose materials that are quick and easy to wipe.

All too much?

Do all our tips feel a bit overwhelming? Don't worry! Look around your kitchen and open the smallest drawer you have. Clean and tidy it. Acquire a nice cutlery tray and start organising. This will take about 14 minutes. And now you've made a start, why not tidy another one?

IKEA® presents FIND IT! PART 2 Kitchen and Food Storage in Ten Homes

All the furnishing solutions in this book were created by the individuals taking part. It's their homes and their ideas. The recipes are also the families' own and IKEA cannot accept any responsibility for them. To make their dreams of kitchen and food storage a reality in the best possible way, interior designers from IKEA helped the families out. IKEA products were used for most of the solutions, and you can find them and other similar products at your IKEA store.

We would love to help you create a better everyday life in your home, and we are sure you'll find something in our range – cabinet units and doors, freestanding cabinets and storage systems, and of course all our hooks, bars, jars, dividers, small shelves and drawer units that help improve the flow in your kitchen.

Some of the solutions contain products that are not in the IKEA range, so we can't accept any responsibility for them.

Remember to read and follow the assembly and safety instructions that come with all IKEA products.

Thanks

to all the families who let us into their kitchens and dining rooms. Thanks for allowing us to look inside your cupboards and drawers, pantries and fridges, and for sharing all your smart, inspiring storage solutions. Also, thanks for the tremendous privilege of sitting down and sharing a meal with you, and even giving us the recipes. A big thank you too to all the photographers and interior designers, writers, graphic designers and everyone else who has contributed to this book in some way.

Here at IKEA we aim to provide as much inspiration as possible, but with minimal impact on the environment. In accordance with our sustainability strategy our books take the environment into account in every stage of production, from the choice of paper to how we distribute our printed material. The book you are holding is printed on paper that meets all the requirements for responsible forestry.
This means, for example, that the paper raw material comes from trees that are certified to originate from a sustainably managed forest. We print using vegetable-based printing inks without solvents.
Read more about how IKEA is working for a sustainable future at www.IKEA.com